NICK FAWCETT

GW00890660

A Pattern
for Prayer

Exploring the Lord's Prayer

kevin
mayhew

First published in 2004 by
KEVIN MAYHEW LTD
Buxhall, Stowmarket, Suffolk, IP14 3BW
E-mail: info@kevinmayhewltd.com

The material in this book first appeared in *Daily Lent
Reflections*.

9 8 7 6 5 4 3 2 1 0
ISBN 1 84417 303 8
Catalogue No. 1500730

Cover design by Angela Selfe
Edited and typeset by Katherine Laidler
Printed and bound in Great Britain

Contents

Introduction

Whenever I find myself struggling in prayer – and that's very often – I turn, almost instinctively, to the Lord's Prayer. Familiar it may be, to the point that we repeat it sometimes parrot-fashion, yet it nonetheless provides a model, offered by Jesus himself, that has stood the test of time. So much is covered in so few words, all of the key ingredients of prayer being found here once you look closely. Above all, there is praise: an acknowledgement of the awesome power and sovereign purpose of God that provides the context in which all prayer should be set. Then there is confession: a recognition of our need for forgiveness coupled with an understanding that this should spill over into forgiving others. Alongside this comes petition and commitment: an entrusting of daily life into God's keeping and a genuine seeking of his will. And, of course, there is finally a concern for others, shown not just in a willingness to forgive but above all in seeking to build God's kingdom, here on earth as it is in heaven.

It would be wrong, however, to treat the Lord's Prayer as though it were spoken in a vacuum. Like everything in the Bible, it needs to be read in context, or, in this case, in *contexts*, for it is recorded twice – in both Luke's and Matthew's Gospels. According to Matthew, whose version we will be following, it formed part of the Sermon on the Mount, whereas according to Luke it was given in response to an enquiry from the disciples as to how they should pray. Must we choose between one or the other? I don't think so, for what could be more natural than for Jesus to repeat this prayer in order to drive home its importance? While Luke emphasises its value as an unparalleled pattern to follow, Matthew highlights the contrast between the simplicity of this prayer and those we can so easily slip into – prayers that sound good yet are often pretentious or superficial.

This book, drawing on material that first appeared in *Daily Lent Reflections*, offers brief thoughts and prayers on Matthew's version of the Lord's Prayer and on the words that precede it. We begin where Jesus began, focusing on the need to make time and space for God in personal devotion. From here we move to a recognition that prayer is not about imposing our wishes on God but about seeking his will and guidance. This leads us into the Lord's Prayer itself – so familiar, so well loved, yet with so many hidden depths still to be explored. If anything in this book helps to make those depths clearer, then it will more than have served its purpose.

NICK FAWCETT

1
Making time

When it comes to prayer, don't make the mistake that
characterises the hypocrites. They like nothing more than to
make a great show of praying, standing conspicuously in the
synagogues or on street corners so that no one can miss them.
The only reward they're going to get is the one they've
obtained already. For your prayers, in contrast,
go into your room, close the door and pray to your Father who
sees into the inner recesses of your mind, and your Father,
who sees in this way, will reward you
Matthew 6:5, 6

Reflection

'Go into your room, close the door and pray to your
Father who sees into the inner recesses of your mind.'
On the face of it, those words merely amplify what Jesus
has already had to say about not parading our virtue in
public, yet there is, I think, another lesson to be drawn
from this passage, and it concerns the importance of set-
ting aside time for quiet prayer and devotion; time, in
other words, to reflect on and commune with God.
Nowhere do we see that better exemplified than in Jesus
himself, in the way he repeatedly drew aside from the
crowds and his disciples to make time and space for
God. Those moments of contemplation and communion
were his lifeblood, nurturing the bond he enjoyed with
his Father, nourishing his spirit, and giving him the
strength, faith and courage he needed to stay true to his
calling. I've no doubt he also made time throughout his
ministry for public worship, but he understood that a

living relationship with God is essentially a personal matter, dependent on moments shared with him if it is to retain its freshness and immediacy.

How does that make you feel: encouraged or disheartened, reassured or troubled, inspired or depressed? The trouble is that most of us find personal devotion difficult, for a host of reasons. Partly, it's a question of time, so many other jobs, responsibilities and demands clamouring for our attention. Partly, it's a question of language, many finding themselves at a loss for words in prayer or struggling to express their true feelings. Partly, it's a question of credibility, some finding it hard to come to terms with apparently unanswered prayer or wrestling with doubts about how God might hear and respond. Partly, also, if we're honest, it's a question of commitment, prayer being very low on our list of priorities compared with innumerable other things we'd rather be doing. The result is that personal devotion tends to go by the board.

So should we feel guilty about this? If we mean by that 'Should we worry that God might punish us for our failure to pray?' then the answer is a resounding 'No!' He may be disappointed at our forgetting him, grieved that we neglect to nurture our side of the relationship, but, whatever the reasons for our failure, his response is to reach out all the more, not to rebuke or chastise but to remind us afresh of his love. Far from eliciting guilt, then, these words of Jesus should give us fresh heart, for underlying them is the assurance that God is always there, waiting to meet with us if only we will respond. Fail to make time for such moments and we do indeed pay a price, for we lose our sense of God's presence and even lose touch with him altogether, but it is a price that we impose on ourselves, not one God demands from us. He is with us now, as he is with us always. However busy you may be, whatever else may need to be done, make time for quiet personal devotion; time to get to know a little better the one who knows you inside out, and loves you just the same.

Prayer

Gracious God,
    whatever else I may forget,
    teach me to remember you
    and to make time for you each day,
    so that I might know you,
    love you
    and serve you better,
    to the glory of your name.
Amen.

2
Simple prayer

*When praying, do not pile up empty words in the way the
Gentiles do, imagining they will be heard because of their
eloquence. Do not copy them, for your Father knows
everything you need before you even ask him*
Matthew 6:7, 8

Reflection

Few people are more annoying than those who never
stop to listen. You know the sort: those who suffer from
verbal diarrhoea, never letting you get a word in edge-
ways. There you are, desperate to chip into the conversa-
tion, to add your twopennyworth, only to be subjected
to a seemingly endless monologue.

I wonder, sometimes, if God ever feels that way about
us for, if your prayers are anything like mine, he too must
often feel bombarded by a barrage of words. We don't do
it consciously; it just ends up happening that way. Not
only is it generally *us* doing all the talking in prayer but the
talking tends also to be all about *us*. We may begin with a
few token words of praise and thanksgiving, but the 'meat'
of our prayers tends to be what concerns us personally:
our needs, desires, troubles and anxieties; our families and
friends; our hopes and aspirations; the routine business of
our daily lives – perhaps with a smattering of intercession
thrown in for good measure. There's nothing inherently
wrong with any of this, of course, except that it's hopelessly
one-sided, just one aspect of what God intends prayer
to be.

The content of such prayers compared to the model Jesus sets out in the Lord's Prayer could hardly be more different. As we will see in the rest of this book, one thing stands out about the latter; it is more about God than us, more about his will than our desires, more about his kingdom than our lives! It begins by acknowledging his greatness and moves on to seek his will, only then turning to us – and even at this point the focus is on the bare essentials of life, the need for forgiveness, and a request for help to stay true to God's way in times of testing. In other words, the prayer is God-centred rather than self-centred.

Surely this is what Jesus had in mind when he advocated simple rather than long-winded prayers. To treat prayer as a shopping list is to misunderstand what it's all about, overlooking the importance of focusing on God, of recognising his greatness and seeking a fuller understanding of his purpose both for our lives and for the world in general. It's about aligning ourselves with God rather than expecting him to align himself with us, about yearning to grow in grace so that we might be more effective in his service – all of which can only happen if we spend time quietly and reflectively in his presence, listening for his voice rather than indulging our own. Does that sound hard? It's not meant to, for God understands the impulse to pour out our concerns, worries and hopes, and I've no doubt he responds wherever and whenever he can, but though such prayer may yield its rewards it will not give us the closeness to God that is prayer's ultimate purpose. Next time you pray, then, spend a little less time talking and a little more listening. You won't be disappointed.

Prayer

Sovereign God,
    when I come to you in prayer,
    instead of bombarding you with words,
    besieging you with requests
    or assaulting you with demands,
    teach me simply to draw near
    and to spend time in your presence
    in quiet communion and companionship.
So may I hear your voice,
    discover your will
    and receive your guidance,
    through Jesus Christ my Lord.
Amen.

3
Our Father

Instead, when you pray, use words like these:
Our Father in heaven . . .
Matthew 6:9a

Reflection

It's often said that we can fail to see what's right under
our very noses, and if ever that was true it must surely
be the case with the Lord's Prayer. It's so familiar to most
of us that, try as we might, we find it well-nigh impossible
not to repeat it parrot-fashion, such that we fail to appre-
ciate its depths or to understand the wonder of what we're
saying. That wonder begins with the very first two words:
Our Father. We're so used to thinking of God in this way that
we scarcely give it another thought, but for the disciples,
hearing Jesus use this form of address for the first time, it
was revolutionary stuff: at once shocking and sensational,
frightening and thrilling. Can any of us truly presume to
approach God with such familiarity – the same God who,
according to the Old Testament, no one can look upon and
live; the God who, hitherto, could only be approached in
the holy of holies via the mediation of the high priest; a
God enthroned over all, righteous and sovereign? Is it
possible to enter into a personal 'family' relationship with
him rather than one based on awe, penitence, even fear? It
must have seemed too good to be true, yet this is precisely
the kind of relationship Jesus goes on making possible day
after day.

Is that how we perceive God? Is that how we approach him? Is that how we understand prayer? We may think so, but before we answer too readily, it might pay to stop and reflect for a moment on parent/child relationships. If things are as they should be, such relationships should be marked by particular qualities: love, trust, respect, commitment, care, affection, and so on. As Jesus says later in this sermon, 'Ask, and you will receive; search, and you will find what you're looking for; knock, and the door will be thrown open. For whoever asks receives, and whoever searches finds, and to whoever knocks, the door will be opened. Would any among you, should your child ask for bread, give a stone? Or if asked for a fish, would you give a snake? If then, you who are flawed know how to give good gifts to your children, how much more will your heavenly Father give good things to those who ask him!' (Matthew 7:7-11)

Children, ideally, should be able to approach their parents in the knowledge that their very presence brings delight; that responding to their needs is a pleasure, not a chore; that their welfare, peace of mind, security and happiness is always of paramount importance. That, says Jesus, is how God feels about us, and that is the confidence in which we can approach him in turn.

All this is not to say, of course, that he will grant every request, come what may; as every parent knows, that would be hopelessly to spoil a child. Nor is it to say that he can *guarantee* happiness; there are limiting factors within this world of ours that, in his wisdom, he has chosen to bind himself by. What it *is* to say is that nothing ultimately will induce him to give us up, any more than, in normal circumstances, loving parents would happily give up a child of their own. The conviction at the heart of our faith, underpinning each moment of every day, is that we are not part of an impersonal meaningless universe but infinitely valued as children by one who calls himself, simply yet wonderfully, 'our Father'.

Prayer

Living God,
    I praise you that though you are above all,
    beyond all,
    before all
    and over all,
    you invite me to call you 'Father';
    the relationship you want me to share with you
    being one of love rather than fear,
    friendship rather than slavery,
    closeness rather than detachment.
For the warmth of your welcome,
    the breadth of your goodness,
    the richness of your grace
    and the wonder of your care,
    Father, I thank you!
Amen.

4
Hallowed be your name

. . . hallowed be your name
Matthew 6:9b

Reflection

'Hallowed be your name' – it's a curious expression, isn't it? When did you last hallow anything? Yet we use those words time and again as we repeat the Lord's Prayer. So what do we mean by them? What, if anything, do we think we're saying when we employ this archaic phrase? To understand that, it might help to think in terms of honouring someone who has died, or perhaps living up to our family name. In the first case, the greatest tribute we can possibly pay is not erecting some plaque or memorial but carrying on the deceased person's work, building upon it, helping to further the things which that individual held dear. In the second case, our aim will be to bring credit upon our family, to reflect well upon them, to keep a tradition alive. Perhaps an even better analogy might be the way a multinational company takes care to safeguard the standing of its brand name. No effort is spared to ensure that this is held in esteem, trusted, associated with all that is best in terms of quality, reliability and service. To hallow, in other words, means to bring glory and honour, admiration and regard.

So it is with the Lord's Prayer, only this time the name in question is God's. When we say 'hallowed be your name' we are not simply asking that everyone may know about God or that his name will be safeguarded from blasphemy. Our prayer, rather, is that everything he stands for may be acknowledged, valued, held high, so that people everywhere might recognise the sort of God he is and the sort of world he yearns for. And that, of course, begins with us. If we who profess his name don't honour him, why should anyone else? If our lives don't testify to his transforming power, why should anyone take notice of the claims of the gospel? If the things we practise do not accord with the things we preach, why should anyone take our message seriously? To pray the Lord's Prayer means, at the very start, to commit ourselves to doing all in our power to honour God's name, striving as far as is humanly possible to make our words and deeds one.

'Hallowed be your name'; it's a curious phrase, undoubtedly, but a powerful one, more powerful than we might have realised – easy to say, but hard to live up to.

Prayer

Loving God,
    teach me that asking for your name to be honoured
    is not enough:
    that, as well as words, I must offer deeds –
    a life that brings you glory
    and that honours everything you stand for,
    all you represent.
So, then, work within me,
    until all I am, think, say and do
    promotes your kingdom
    and redounds to your honour,
    through Jesus Christ my Lord.
Amen.

5
On earth, as it is in heaven

May your kingdom come and your will be done on earth,
as it is in heaven
Matthew 6:10

Reflection

At the last General Election in the UK a disturbing trend
became all too apparent: people across the country, and
especially young people, are losing interest in politics.
Does that matter? I think it does, for a variety of reasons.
It suggests first that people are disillusioned with polit-
icians, no longer trusting them as they once did; most
people, in fact, barely believing what they say at all. Rightly
or wrongly, Westminster in particular has become associated with 'spin' and broken promises, with many words
disguising little action. If that's a problem in itself, perhaps
a greater one is that ever-fewer people appear to believe in
the political process, and thus fewer still are becoming
involved in the decision-making forums of society. Perhaps
most troubling of all is the implication that people have
given up believing things can change, resigning themselves
instead to making the best of a bad job.

As Christians, similar cynicism can strike at the very
heart of our faith. We talk of the kingdom of God, and
we repeat the words of the Lord's Prayer, 'your kingdom
come', but we conveniently forget the line that follows
this: 'on earth, as it is in heaven'. Can that ever begin
to happen, we ask ourselves? One look at the ills that
beset our world would seem to suggest otherwise. Some
perhaps have occasionally dared to dream – at the end of

a world war perhaps, at the inception of the welfare state, at the close of the Cold War, and so forth – but for each evil ended another has begun, and for every new dawn there seems to be a corresponding twilight. Is there any prospect of witnessing God's kingdom here on earth? It would be an idealist indeed who expects to see it in his or her lifetime, but that should not stop us from trying to bring it closer. And that takes us back to what I was saying earlier about politics. People may have lost faith in the established channels of debate but not all have given up believing things can change. Many have resorted to what is termed 'direct action', whether that means a march of protest, a peace camp or an anti-roads sit-in. We may applaud such efforts or condemn them, depending on our point of view and the methods employed, but no one can deny the commitment many show to their cause, or question the firmness of their convictions.

As followers of Christ we are called to direct action of a different sort. Every deed of love, act of service, extension of forgiveness, gesture of compassion or expression of faith contributes to the fulfilment of God's purpose, the promotion of his kingdom here on earth. These may not seem much and their impact may appear small, but they are a beginning; as the old proverb has it: 'drop by drop fills the bucket'. One thing is certain, if we want to see change, we have to contribute to make it happen. To pray 'your kingdom come' is not simply to express pious hopes about the distant future but to commit ourselves to the present. It means, instead of asking when that kingdom may come, asking rather what *we* personally are doing to help bring it nearer.

Prayer

Sovereign God,
    instead of promoting my purposes
    may I seek yours;
    instead of furthering my own ends
    may I pursue *your* interests;
    instead of striving to achieve my goals
    may I labour first to build your kingdom.
Teach me what it means to pray 'your will be done',
    and help me not just to *say* those words
    but also to *mean* them.
Amen.

6
Daily bread

Give us each day our daily bread
Matthew 6:11

Reflection

'And this,' said the couple, showing me round their
delightful and luxurious cottage, 'was another answer to
prayer. We asked God to provide the right place and this
is what he's given.' They were evidently sincere, and there
was no way anyone could fault their commitment, yet I
couldn't help but question whether prayer had anything
whatsoever to do with their plush new surroundings.
Does God really provide us with the perks of life, whether
that is a new home, good job, decent income or so forth?
If so, it's hard not to ask why he allows others to face
homelessness, hunger, poverty and all manner of other
privations. The idea sits even less easily with the repeated
call of Jesus in the Gospels to renounce material blessings,
and least comfortably of all with the words of the Lord's
Prayer: 'Give us each day our daily bread'. The meaning
here is straightforward enough: not 'give us a sumptuous
feast, a slap-up meal'; not even 'give us a good feed'; but
give us enough of what we *need*. There is admittedly a
strand of teaching in the Old Testament that equates
prosperity with God's blessing, labelled the Deutero-
nomic history by biblical theologians, but such a belief was
forcibly countered by other Old Testament writers, not least
in the book of Job.

All this is not to say we shouldn't be thankful for the
blessings life puts our way, whether through our own

efforts, good fortune or accident of birth. Everything ultimately belongs to God, and a proper sense of gratitude will spill over into a responsible and generous stewarding of what he has given, but we should, I think, be cautious in postulating a direct link between material blessing and answered prayer; and even more cautious about ever praying for such blessing. The model Jesus gives is, as we have seen, altogether different: 'Give us each day our daily bread'. In other words, give us what we need to get by; not what we would like but what we can't do without. It is a request that fits in with everything Jesus has to say elsewhere about treasures on earth and in heaven, about serving God and money, about seeking above all else the kingdom of God and his righteousness. Interestingly, this single line comprises the sole instance within the Lord's Prayer of asking God to provide for our personal needs. The only other requests made are for forgiveness, protection from temptation and deliverance from evil; that is to say, each concerned simply with faithful discipleship rather than personal gain.

How do your prayers compare to this? How much do they focus on God providing your wishes and how much on *you* fulfilling *his* will? Faith is not a celestial investment scheme, guaranteeing lucrative dividends in the here and now. It does not offer access to some heavenly slot machine, promising a bumper payout if we put in sufficient prayer and supplication and come up with the right devotional combination. It is rather the conviction that, whatever we face, God will sufficiently meet our needs – physically, emotionally and spiritually – for us to stay true to him and to persevere in his service until our journey's end. Then, and only then, are we guaranteed his unreserved, unlimited and unending blessing.

Prayer

Faithful God,
    teach me to be content with what I *have*
    rather than to bemoan what I *wish* I had;
    to focus on what I *need*
    rather than dwell on what I *want*;
    to appreciate the *essentials* of life
    rather than constantly to crave its *luxuries*.
Help me, in other words,
    to celebrate the things that matter,
    and to let go of those that don't.
In Christ's name I pray.
Amen.

7
The key to forgiveness

*. . . and forgive our mistakes as we forgive those
who wrong us. If you forgive others their mistakes,
your heavenly Father will forgive you likewise;
but if you refuse to forgive them
your Father will withhold forgiveness from you in turn*
Matthew 6:12, 14, 15

Reflection

To understand what forgiveness means in terms of our
relationship with God, I want you to picture yourself in a
somewhat sticky situation. Imagine that you've lost con-
centration while driving, and have been pulled over by
the police for speeding. You weren't just a little over the
speed limit but way beyond it, so you have no reason
whatsoever to expect any clemency, despite your evident
shame and profuse apologies. Perhaps if your licence were
clean you might just possibly hope for a stern telling
off and nothing more, but no, you've been guilty of the
same offence and numerous others on countless occasions
before. Little wonder, then, that you fear the worst. But
what's this? Impossible surely! Without even wanting to
see any documentation the policeman is sending you on
your way, with just a cautionary word. Amazing!

Whether it would be good for police to show such
leniency is questionable to say the least, but that is the
sort of forgiveness God shows us. Though we repeatedly
transgress against him, stepping hopelessly outside his
commandments, he is always willing to give us another
chance.

Though we fail him time and again, if we acknowledge our mistakes and genuinely seek forgiveness, then, as far as he's concerned, there is no record of them; it's as though they've never been.

So that's it then? We just need to express sorrow to receive forgiveness? Well, yes . . . and no. It all depends on what we mean by being sorry, for in relation to God such sorrow needs to be active as well as passive. True remorse shows itself in a desire to change, to show that our expression of regret is more than empty words; and, according to Jesus, the best way to do that – perhaps, even, the only way – is to forgive others in turn.

Is God's forgiveness conditional, then, on our forgiving others? It can't be, for if it were we'd all be in a sorry pass. Moreover, it would make God's love dependent on works rather than faith. Yet, if nothing else, we must surely aim to forgive, even if we fail. If the intention to do so isn't there, then we deny ourselves God's forgiveness, not because he withholds it but because we haven't grasped what it means and so are unable to make it ours. So next time you come before God, seeking his mercy, begging for pardon, stop and ask yourself whether others are seeking the same from you, and whether you've really understood what forgiveness is all about.

Prayer

Gracious God,
    remind me afresh each day
    of your love that goes on reaching out,
    your mercy that knows no bounds,
    your patience that is never exhausted
    and your goodness that nothing can exhaust,
    and so may I live each day in constant celebration,
    responding to your great faithfulness
    in joyful service.
Amen.

8

Rescue us from evil

*Save us from falling prey to temptation,
and rescue us from evil*
Matthew 6:13

Reflection

'Rescue us from evil' – we'd all say Amen to that, wouldn't we? But what are we actually asking for? Can prayer ever inoculate us against suffering and sorrow, heartache and hardship? The answer, of course, is no. Tragedy afflicts the Christian as much as anyone else. Pain is just as real, illness just as likely, and, ultimately, death as inevitable for us as it is for the next person. If we suppose saying a prayer each day is going to protect us from such things we are sadly deluded. God, I am sure, does not wish such things upon us for a moment, but they are part of life as we know it, an inescapable facet of being human. So why does Jesus teach us to pray, 'rescue us from evil'? To understand that we need to recognise first that the evil he has in mind is something altogether different, referring instead to anything and everything that might separate us from God. This may come in various guises: in the temptation to turn our back flagrantly on God and flout his will; in more subtle pressures to compromise and dilute our faith, unwittingly denying it through an imperceptible but inexorable blurring of the edges; in circumstances and events that apparently contradict belief, causing us to question our faith or lose it completely. These pressures and temptations are stronger and more common than we might imagine, and however committed we might think ourselves to be, none of us, through our own efforts, can be confident of standing firm. We need God's strength and support; his Spirit within to guide, counsel, equip and inspire; his grace to lift us up when we stumble and encourage us forward once again.

We cannot claim any special exemption from the challenges life might dish out, but we can claim God's help in meeting them, the assurance of his presence by our side through the darkest valley and deepest shadows. *He* will not let go of us but *we* can all too easily let go of him. That is why we pray 'rescue us from evil' – both to remind ourselves of the threat we're up against and to seek God's help in meeting it.

Prayer

Living God,
   I know my weakness all too well:
   my lack of faith,
   my limited courage,
   my flawed commitment.
I know, should testing come,
   that I will struggle to hold on,
   my discipleship less secure than I would wish.
Protect me, then, from evil,
   safeguard me from temptation,
   and deliver me from times of trial,
   through Jesus Christ my Lord.
Amen.

9
Prayer in context

*For the kingdom, the power and the glory are yours,
now and for evermore. Amen*
Matthew 6:13b
(added in some ancient manuscripts only)

Reflection

Have you ever watched a favourite film from which a
scene has been cut? You sit there, taking it all in, only
suddenly to realise that something is missing, what to
you was an essential ingredient no longer there. The film
still holds together – indeed, someone watching it for the
first time would be oblivious to the omission – but to
you it just doesn't feel quite right.

There was something of that feeling, I think, among
those who first read Matthew's version of the Lord's
Prayer. It represented faithfully the words that Jesus had
taught, but it wasn't quite the prayer they had become
used to repeating. Why? Because just about every prayer
used at the time would end with a doxology, an affirm-
ation of faith, a statement summing up the sovereign
nature of God to whom the prayer was offered. And so it
was that various copies of Matthew's Gospel appeared
with a line added to this prayer: additional words that will
be familiar to every Christian and many others today:
'For the kingdom, the power and the glory are yours, now
and for evermore. Amen.'

Was that just an arbitrary embellishment, a postscript
added as an afterthought? I don't think so. It was included
not just because the prayer *felt* incomplete but because

those who prayed it believed it actually *was*. Possibly they thought Matthew had forgotten the exact words Jesus used or perhaps they felt that this was the way Jesus expected us to conclude in prayer. Either way, the addition is important, for it sets the context not just for this prayer, nor even for the Sermon on the Mount in general, but for the whole of Jesus' life and ministry. He has spoken about God's kingdom and helped to bring it closer here on earth; he has referred to temptation and evil that might deflect us from the path of discipleship; he has touched on the need to align ourselves to God's will if we would truly see it done – and each of these are points we do well to remember. But there is a danger of us losing sight of the fact that though God's will may currently be frustrated, though his kingdom is not yet realised, and though temptation strikes and evil seems victorious, the future is secure, all things ultimately in his hands. The kingdom, power and glory are indeed his, now and always; he will not fail.

We can apply that further to everything Jesus has to say in the Sermon on the Mount – the overall context for this prayer – much of which can seem daunting, hopelessly beyond us. How can we love our enemies, go the extra mile, be salt and light to the world, overcome our self-centredness, and show works that correspond to our faith? The answer of course, is that we can't. If it was down to us alone, we wouldn't have a hope of success or anywhere to turn to for help. But we, like everyone else, are finally in God's hands. He is able to use us beyond our every expectation and to forgive when we fail, patiently and lovingly moulding us into his people, however many times he needs to refashion the clay and start again. The kingdom, power and glory are his; so also, thank God, are we.

Prayer

Lord of all,
    teach me to focus not on myself but on you,
    and may that put all else in perspective,
    so that I may happily leave every aspect of life
    safely in your hands.
In Christ's name I pray.
Amen.